Jokes & Quotes
for Speeches

Jokes & Quotes for Speeches

CASSELL
ILLUSTRATED

First published in Great Britain in 2006
by Cassell Illustrated
A division of Octopus Publishing Group Ltd
2–4 Heron Quays
London E14 4JP

Text and design copyright © 2006 Cassell Illustrated
Selected text taken from Speechmakers' Bible, published in 2005 by Cassell
Illustrated. Additional text supplied by JMS Books.

A CIP catalogue record for this book is available from the British Library.

ISBN-13: 978-1-844035-19-9
ISBN-10: 1-844035-19-0

Printed and bound in the United Kingdom

Contents

Introduction

'You'll have to make a speech!' are words you may wish never to hear. It may be for a wedding, a business lunch, an informal group, the Parent-teacher Association, a school speech day, or an informal family celebration. But have no fear. Whatever your experience, and despite what you may think, speechmaking can be fun and this book is here to help you.

There are two principal factors involved in the making of a public speaker: there is the person who makes and delivers the speech, and there is the message that the speaker delivers. Some people are naturally more extrovert than others and thrive on audience attention, while others shy away from it and may remember stumbling over a passage they had to read aloud in school. The greatest fear of a speechmaker is often that their audience will be bored by their speech, and so incorporating a joke, quote or story is a favoured way of livening it up a bit. However, finding appropriate jokes and quotes to include is often a problem, and this book will provide you with some of the content, reference material or raw materials for your speeches in the form of jokes, quotes, stories and anecdotes.

An extensive selection of jokes and quotes are included here, together with advice on how to choose personal anecdotes in your speech. The jokes and quotes are given in subject order and many of the suggestions can be adapted for other situations. If you are searching for material for a wedding speech, for example, do not just refer to the section on weddings and anniversaries. Suitable material might also be found in the section on birthdays. More general jokes and quotes are worth considering for any type of speech, as even areas that have nothing to do with your subject may provide the spark that will lift your speech from predictable run-of-the-mill to something your audience will remember for a long time to come.

When making any kind of speech, there are certain things you will need to remember for your speech to be a success:

• Don't allow yourself to be overwhelmed by the concept of 'making a speech'. Instead, think of it rather as welcoming supportive, friendly people to the event and entertaining them for a few minutes – a sort of extended conversation that just happens to be with a larger than usual group of people.

• Don't leave things to the last minute, and unless you have a special gift for excellent and improvised public speaking, make sure you prepare what you are going to say well in advance.

- Don't underestimate your audience or, indeed, over-estimate them – in age, experience, tolerance and understanding of your language or humour. Not everyone will be as familiar with the subject as you. There may be grannies and children present, so if using humour, keep it in proportion.

- Don't look down when you talk, don't whisper and don't shout, don't swear too much and don't improvise unless you feel really confident.

- Don't make your speech a series of loosely connected quotations from famous or other people. If you have written your own poem, don't perform it unless it has been read and vetted first.

- Don't forget that this speech is about the occasion and your relationship to the person/people involved. It is not a speech about you. It is not a vehicle for self-promotion or an audition for a reality show. Don't confuse 'eye contact' with 'I contact'.

Regardless of whether you choose to include a joke, quote, story or anecdote, it is vital that it is used properly and not just peppered into your speech. The following framework may help:

Item–Point–Relevance

Item: When using 'item–point–relevance', first we use the item, i.e. we tell the joke, recount the story or anecdote, show the picture or quote the quote.

Point: Often speakers are guilty of using quotes, humour stories, etc. without explaining why they are using them. For example, if a father was telling a story about his daughter's persistence in life in a father-of-the-bride speech it can often help to complete the circle by explaining the point of the story.

Relevance: Having told the story and/or explained the point, it may be necessary then to explain the relevance of that point within the overall context of the speech or to the audience who are listening to the speech.

When using 'item–point–relevance', it is key that its use is not too structured and rigid and avoids the direct use of the three words. When used effectively this completes the circle of a good story by ensuring that the point you are making is clearly understood and the audience can see how it relates to your speech and the occasion overall.

An example of this could be:

Item
'Carl Jung said: 'The meeting of two personalities is like the contact of two chemical substances; if there is any reaction, both are transformed.' '

Point
'I believe that what Jung meant was that when two people meet and connect, who they are changes forever as a result of that meeting.'

Relevance
'Certainly, when Chris and Sue met there was a reaction and both have been transformed forever. This fantastic transformation has managed to bring out the best in both of them as they are blooming with happiness, confidence and kindness.'

chapter 1

Jokes

Jokes and humour can add to the interest and quality of your speeches, but before using them you should apply this pre-joke checklist to avoid coming badly unstuck:

- Are you funny/good at telling jokes? Beware of a difference between perception and reality. Just because you've been told you are a funny guy does not mean you are a good joke teller. Get some feedback from a neutral, direct and candid person. If the answer's not a firm and immediate 'yes', then leave it out. For those of us that are not fantastic joke tellers, personal anecdotes or stories are often a much better solution.

- Is this the right occasion to be telling a joke? Obviously, a funeral is frequently not the best place for humour. But even more mundane situations should be treated carefully with regard to humour. If a speaker is addressing a group of people who have under-performed or failed to deliver, it may deliver the message that what they are doing or have done is OK.

- Is this joke appropriate for this audience? Sex, politics and religion are all sensitive subjects. This is not to say that jokes about them should never be used. The point is, will it go down well with this particular audience? You must dry-run jokes with typical audience members. Just because it had your 20-something mates in stitches doesn't mean it will have the same effect upon an older audience. Sometimes the humour just won't translate.

- Is this the right moment of the speech for a joke? Humour has its place within speeches. It is often good as an engagement item near the beginning or during the main body. But if you have spent time building up strong feelings and emotions in your audience by, for example, talking seriously about love at a wedding, think carefully about blowing this good work apart with a sledgehammer joke.

- Is the audience likely to have heard the joke before? Be careful about borrowing humour from the media as it could well fall flat if everyone has heard it before.

Once you have ticked off this list, you then have licence to try to be funny, but how do you pull it off?

Here are a few guidelines to jokes within speeches:

- Focus on how you tell the joke: As Frank Carson says: 'It's the way I tell 'em.' Good delivery of jokes is a prerequisite to telling them at all.

- Timing: Never, ever rush the punch line.

- Practise, practise and practise again. Knowing the joke inside out will free you up to focus on your delivery.

- Make it personal: Substitute audience members' names for the names of the people in the joke.

- Concealed jokes: Try starting your joke in your normal speech style and audience members won't see it for what it is. Then when the light bulb comes on the impact is magnified.

Below are a selection of jokes and amusing one-liners listed under theme and subject matter; they can be adapted, as necessary, for different occasions.

Age

My wild oats have turned into prunes and All Bran.

I finally got my head together; now my body is falling apart.

It is easier to get older than it is to get wiser.

These days, I spend a lot of time thinking about the hereafter... I go somewhere to get something and then wonder what I'm here after.

Old musicians never die, they just get played out.
Old pacifists never die, they just go to peaces.
Old digital photographers never die, they just go to old focus homes.
Old 3mm photographers never die, they just cease developing.
Old pilots never die, they just buzz off suddenly.
Old pilots from Helsinki never die, they just vanish into Finn Air.
Old policemen never die, they just cop out.
Old plumbers never die, they just go down the drain.
Old hippies never die, they just smell that way.
Old skiers never die, they just go downhill fast.
Old window cleaners never die, they just kick the bucket.
Old garage workers never die, they just re-tire.
Old golfers never die, they just lose their drive.

You know you are getting old when you feel like the morning after but you haven't been anywhere the night before (or at least you don't think so...)

You know you are getting old when your little black book is full of names beginning with Doctor...

You know you are getting old when your belt won't buckle but your knees do it without the least hesitation.

You know when you are getting old when you sink your teeth into a nice juicy steak – and they stay there.

You know when you are getting old when you still think you know all the answers, but you can't remember the questions.

Age is a high price to pay for maturity.

The older you get, the better you realize you must have been if only you could remember.

I think, therefore I am.
I doubt, therefore I might be.
I am old, therefore I can't remember.

Be nice to your children. They will choose your nursing home.

Birthdays

The only sure way to remember your wife's birthday is to forget it once.

If you forget your wife's birthday, tell her it is hard to remember because she never looks any older.

When he lit all the candles on his birthday cake, three people collapsed from the heat.

You know you are getting older when someone usually calls the fire department after you light the candles on your birthday cake.

A true friend remembers your birthday, but forgets your age.

I never forget my wife's birthday. It is usually the day after she reminds me about it.

My wife wanted something studded with diamonds for her birthday. So I bought her a pack of playing cards...

How does Moby Dick celebrate his birthday? He has a whale of a party!

My wife told me she didn't put candles on my birthday cake because she wanted to save the environment...

It is proven that the celebration of birthdays is healthy – statistics show that those people who celebrate the most birthdays live longest.

Children

There's only one way I can make my children notice that I've got home from work – I walk in front of the television set.

Kids in the back seat cause accidents, but accidents in the back seat cause kids.

A statistician's wife had twins. He was delighted. He rang the priest who was also delighted and told him to bring them to the church on Sunday to have them baptized. 'No,' said the statistician. 'Baptize one. We will keep the other as a control.'

A friend of ours has three monsters and she is always moaning about them. One day, I asked her if she could go back in time, would she do it all over again and have children. 'Oh yes, of course I would,' she replied, 'but not the same ones.'

After we got home from the hospital I suggested to my husband that he should try his hand at changing nappies. 'I'm busy at the moment,' he replied, 'I'll do the next one.' So, later that day, I asked him if he could do the next change. 'I meant the next baby, not the next nappy,' he explained gently.

The best way to advise your children is to ask what they want to do and then tell them not to do it.

Money isn't everything but it helps persuade the kids to keep in touch.

Things not to say to your wife during childbirth:
> 'Honey, is there anything in the refrigerator for dinner?'
> 'Are you sure you aren't having twins? Your stomach looks like there's another one in there.'
> 'Can you just check I cut the right cord?'
> 'I didn't need an epidural when I twisted my ankle – what's the big deal?'
> 'Do you really have to swear so much? Try to relax and enjoy the moment.'

When you have your first baby you rush out and buy designer maternity clothes as soon as you hear you are pregnant.
When you have your second baby, you wear your usual clothes for as long as possible.
When you have your third, your maternity clothes are your usual ones.

The 'joy of parenthood' is what washes over you like a warm wave – when the kids are in bed.

What are the only two things small children willingly share? Your age and their communicable diseases.

If I wanted to hear the pitter-patter of tiny feet, I would have put shoes on my cats.

Why is it American men only call their sons after themselves? Has anyone ever heard of a Marybelle Junior?

Christmas

Good King Wenceslas went into a well-known pizza
  parlour.
'The usual, sir?' said the waiter.
'Yes,' said Good King Wenceslas. 'Deep pan, crisp, and
  even.'

What do snowmen eat for breakfast? Snowflakes.

What did Adam say on the day before Christmas?
'It's Christmas, Eve.'

What do you call people who are afraid of Santa?
Claustrophobic.

What do elves learn at kindergarten? The elf-abet.

Why did Santa's little helper go to the therapist?
Because he had low elf esteem.

Which of the following expressions do you see most
often at Christmas: Goodwill to Men, Peace on Earth or
Batteries Not Included?

What do lawyers call Santa's helpers? Subordinate
Clauses.

What does Santa do with his helpers if they eat too
many mince pies? He sends them to an elf farm.

Why doesn't Santa have any children? Because he only
comes once a year.

Cigarettes

I decided to give up cigarettes in two stages. First I'm going to give up smoking my cigarettes… and then I'll give up smoking other people's.

A man walks into a service station and buys a packet of cigarettes. He pulls one out and lights up. The cashier says, 'Excuse me sir, but you can't smoke in here.' The man replies, 'Don't you think it is rather stupid that I can buy cigarettes here but I can't smoke them?' The cashier replies, 'Not at all, sir. We also sell contraceptives.'

I think I am very broad-minded with my son and his friends when they ask if they can smoke in the house. I tell them they are free to do whatever they like, whenever they like, for as long as they like – on the doorstep.

My father gave me some very good advice about smoking. Have your first cigarette on the same day you kiss your first girlfriend – but just afterwards. You will never have time for tobacco again.

True story: Having bought several fabulously expensive cigars, a man from North Carolina, America, insured them against fire. He then smoked them and filed a claim against the insurance company, stating that he had lost them in a series of small fires. They refused to pay and he sued. The judge said that since the cigars were insured against fire, the company were obliged to pay. They duly coughed up, but then arrested him on 24 separate counts of arson.

Drink

A drunk staggers into a Catholic church, enters a confessional box, sits down but says nothing. The priest coughs a few times to get his attention, but the drunk just sits there. Finally, the priest pounds three times on the wall. The drunk mumbles: 'Ain't no use knockin', there's no paper on this side either.'

A glass of [wine/whisky/champagne] is said to cure all sorts of ills, such as the common cold. All you need is a candle and a bottle of [wine/whisky/champagne]. Light the candle, drink the first glass and wait five minutes. Drink another glass and wait, still watching the candle. Keep drinking until you see three candles, then snuff out the middle one and go to sleep.

A drunk was hauled into court. 'Mister,' the judge began, 'you've been brought here for drinking.'
'Great,' the drunk exclaimed, 'When do we get started?'

Warnings that should be put on alcohol bottles:
Consumption of alcohol can:
- make you think you are whispering.
- make you think you can sing.
- make you think your ex really wants you to call him/her at 4am.
- make you forget who you are, where you are, why you are naked, why you were tied to a tree by your male friends.
- make you think you are irresistibly charming, handsome and equipped with wings.

Brenda O'Malley is home making dinner, as usual, when Tim Finnegan arrives at her door. 'Brenda, may I come in?' he asks. 'I've somethin' to tell ya.'
'Of course you can come in, you're always welcome, Tim. But where's my husband?'
'That's what I'm here to be tellin' ya, Brenda. There was an accident down at the Guinness brewery...'
'Oh, God no!' cries Brenda. 'Please don't tell me...'
'I must, Brenda. Your husband Seamus is dead and gone. I'm sorry.' Finally, Brenda looks up at Tim.
'How did it happen, Tim?'
'It was terrible, Brenda. He fell into a vat of Guinness Stout and drowned.'
'Oh my dear Jesus! But you must tell me true, Tim. Did he at least go quickly?'
'Well, no Brenda... no. Fact is, he got out three times to have a pee.'

A man walks into the room and tells his wife he is off to the pub and she should put her coat on. She is delighted to be invited to a social event with her husband, puts on her newly purchased full-length fake fur coat and heads for the door. 'What are you doing, love? I just meant I was going to turn the heating off.'

How many footballers does it take to change a light bulb? Eleven. One to hold the bulb and the rest of the team to drink until the room spins.

Two Irishmen walk into a bar...you would think one of them would have seen it!

What do you call a drunk who works in an upholstery shop? A recovering alcoholic.

A man goes to the doctor and complains he has a drinking problem. 'What is it?' asks the doctor.
'When I am drinking whisky I have two hands but only one mouth.'

My wife went to the doctor and he told her to stay away from alcohol and cigarettes. Now she's filing for divorce.

My wife is a lawyer and a workaholic. She can stay up all night working on a case of champagne.

A man walks into a bar with a lump of tarmac under his arm and says, 'Pint please, and one for the road.'

Three 80-year-old ladies are walking down the street.
One says, 'Golly, it is windy today!'
'No, today is Thursday,' says the second lady.
'So am I, let's find a pub,' says the third.

Men are like fine wine. They start out as grapes, and it is our job to stamp and tread upon them and keep them in the dark until they mature into something we would like to have dinner with.

Women are like fine wine. They start out all fresh, sweet, fruity, intoxicating and refreshing, and then they turn full-bodied, become sour and vinegary and end up giving us a headache.

A man walks into his local and asks for a beer. After drinking it, he looks into his wallet and asks for another beer. After downing that one, he looks in his wallet and orders another. His friend sees him doing this and asks if he would like to borrow some money. When his friend says no, he asks him why he keeps looking in his wallet before ordering another beer. 'I have got a photo of my wife in there. When she starts to look attractive, I will go home,' he replies.

What is a wife's favourite wine?
'Why didn't you ring me to say you were going to be late?'

What is a husband's favourite wine?
'How can you possibly need another pair of shoes?'

A thief gets stopped by a policeman. 'What's that in your bag?' says the officer. 'It's a bottle of wine. I got it for my wife,' replies the thief. 'Good trade,' says the policeman.

A vicar gets stopped for speeding on a country lane. The policeman smells alcohol on his breath and sees an empty bottle on the floor of the car.
'Have you been drinking, sir?' asks the officer.
'Just water,' replies the priest.
'So why do I smell wine?' asks the policeman.
'Praise the Lord! He's done it again!' answers the priest.

Exercise

The trouble with jogging is that by the time you realize you are not fit enough to do it, you've got a long walk home.

If God wanted me to touch my toes, he would have put them on my knees.

My personal trainer told me to touch my toes. But I don't have that kind of relationship with my feet so I asked if I could just wave instead?

I told my husband to get a six pack and he went to the off licence.

How do you get your husband to do sit-ups? Put the remote control between his toes.

My husband is in shape. Round is a shape, after all.

Inside me is a thin, fit person struggling to escape but I can usually sedate her/him with four or five chocolate chip muffins.

The advantage of exercising every day is that you die healthier.

The older you get, the tougher it is to part your body and your fat as by then they are really firm friends.

I tried jogging but my thighs kept rubbing together and setting my underwear on fire.

I told my husband it was important to stay in shape. He started walking 5 miles a day when he was 40 and now he is 50 and we have no idea where he is.

Every time I feel like doing some exercise, I lie down until the urge passes.

I keep fit by going out:
- five nights on the trot.
- six nights running.

My idea of exercise is:
- to leap to conclusions.
- to jump ship.
- to skip. I skip gym classes, mostly.
- to beat around the bush.
- to wade through my paperwork.
- to balance the books.

I haven't got time to exercise. I get exhausted by:
- adding fuel to the fire.
- running around in circles.
- picking up the pieces.
- making mountains out of mole hills.
- social climbing.
- pulling out all the stops.
- putting my foot in my mouth.

How does a physicist exercise? By pumping ion...

What is a runner's favourite subject? Jography...

Fathers

What do you call two people who embarrass you in front of your friends? Your parents.

When I was young, if a father put a roof over his family's head he was a success. Now it takes a roof, pool, deck and 3-car garage, and that is just the holiday home.

When I was young, I used to stand up if my father walked in the room. Now my kids just tell me I am invading their space.

Everything I know about sex, drugs, rock 'n' roll and the internet...I learned from my son.

I am so proud of my children. They raised £1000 for their school and now none of our relatives ever ring us back.

Things you will never hear a father say:
> 'Your mother and I are going away for the weekend.
> Why not throw a party?'
> 'No son of mine is going to live under my roof without
> a nose ring and belly button piercing.'
> 'Why bother looking for a job? Here's £60.'
> 'I noticed your friends are hostile, rude and don't
> wash much. I like that.'
> 'Let's ask this lady on the pavement for directions. I
> am not sure of the way.'

Never raise your hand to your kids. It leaves you far too exposed.

Ben's mum dragged him in front of his father during the soccer game.
'Talk to your son,' she said, 'He refuses to obey a word I say.'
'Ben, how dare you disobey your mother?' said his father, 'That is my job!'

I have always told my children not to marry for money. You can borrow it more cheaply.

My son asked me what my wife and I use as contraceptives. 'Nudity,' I replied.

My son asked me what the difference was between a girlfriend and a wife, and I told him about 2 stone.

My best friend asked me what my son was taking in college. I replied, 'Everything I have.'

Golf

Two men were out golfing. As one was about to take his shot, a funeral procession drove by the golf course. The man stopped what he was doing, put down his club, took off his hat and placed it over his heart. His partner was moved by this and said: 'That's the nicest thing I've ever seen you do!' The man looked back at him and said: 'Well, it's the least I could do after 20 years of marriage...'

An octogenarian's golf game was hampered by his poor eyesight. His doctor teamed him up with a nonagenarian with perfect vision. The 80-year old hit the first ball and asked his companion if he could see where it landed.
'Yes,' said the 90-year-old.
'Where?' asked the younger man.
'Sorry, I just can't remember!' came the reply.

A golf club walks into a bar and orders a pint of beer. The barman refuses to serve the golf club. 'Why not?' it asks. 'You'll be driving later,' replies the barman.

What do you call a blonde golfer with an IQ of 125?
A foursome.

As a golfer I always find that my best round of golf is followed almost immediately by my worst. The probability of the latter increases with the number of people you tell about the former.

My wife said I had to give up golf or she would leave me. I don't miss her as much as I thought I would.

Once upon a time, a guy asked a girl to marry him. She said no and the guy lived happily ever after and played golf every day. That just proves my life is no fairytale after all.

My wife agrees with Winston Churchill, who said that playing golf was like chasing a quinine pill around a cow pasture. I tell her there is nothing better than fresh air, blue skies, a beautiful partner and a good round of golf, although the first three aren't that important.

A married man and his secretary are having an affair. They decide to leave the office early one day and go to the secretary's apartment for an afternoon of love. Exhausted, they fall asleep and don't wake up until 9pm that night. They get dressed quickly and the man asks his secretary to take his shoes and rub them in the grass. She thinks it is a pretty weird request but does it anyway. The man finally gets home and his wife meets him at the door. She is very upset and asks him where he has been. The husband says, 'I can't tell a lie. I am having an affair with my secretary and we left work early, went to her place and made love all afternoon. Then we fell asleep, and that is why I am late.' His wife looks at him, looks at his shoes and says, 'You can't fool me. I can see grass stains all over your shoes. You've been playing golf again, haven't you?'

Life
I started out with nothing, and I still have most of it.

All reports are in; life is now officially unfair.

If all is not lost, where is it?

Some days you're the dog; some days you're the tree.

It's hard to make a comeback when you haven't been anywhere.

The only time the world beats a path to your door is when you're in the bathroom.

When I'm finally holding all the cards, why does everyone decide to play chess?

My job is secure. Nobody else wants it.

Sometimes I wish life came with subtitles.

Always be sincere, even if you don't mean it.

A clear conscience is just the result of a poor memory.

Every time I think the world is moving too fast, I go and queue up in the Post Office.

Have you ever noticed that wrong numbers are never busy?

Love and Romance

If you love something, set it free.
If it comes back, it was always yours and shall remain so.
If it never returns, it was never yours.
If it sits in the living room, messes up your stuff, eats your food, uses your telephone, comes home late, never washes up or does the ironing, and never looks like it wants to be set free, you gave birth to it or married it.

I asked a statistician for her phone number and she gave me an estimate.

I like my men like my coffee. Finely ground and in the freezer.

I like my women like my coffee. Cold and bitter.

I am one bad relationship away from getting 20 cats.

I wanted to fall in love with a psychic but she left the country before we met.

My girlfriend asked if I would buy her a ring if we got engaged. I said I would if she gave me her mobile number.

I filled in a form at a dating agency recently describing my ideal woman. She would be petite, cute, into water sports and group activities and looked good in black. The agency came back and told me I should marry a penguin.

When my friend's future son-in-law came to ask for his daughter's hand in marriage, he asked him if he was earning enough to support a family. The young man replied confidently that he indeed was but his bright young face fell a mile when his future father-in-law said, 'Think carefully now, son. There are twelve of us.'

How does a man impress a woman on a date? Compliment her, buy her dinner, bring her flowers, listen to her, take her home, kiss her on the cheek.

How does a woman impress a man on a date? Wear a short skirt and bring a case of beer.

Love is blind, but marriage is an eye-opener.

When my daughter broke up with her boyfriend she asked me what she should do about returning the gifts he had given her. I told her to send back the stuffed animals, the letters, the photographs, but to keep the jewellery for sentimental reasons.

Marriage

A little girl went to a wedding. Afterwards, she asked her mother why the bride changed her mind. 'What do you mean?' responded her mother. 'Well, she went down the aisle with one man, and came back with another.'

I like the story of the woman who had an artist paint a portrait of her covered with jewels. Her explanation: 'If I die and my husband remarries, I want his next wife to go crazy looking for the jewels.'

In the first year of marriage, the man speaks and the woman listens.
In the second year, the woman speaks and the man listens.
In the third year, they both speak and the neighbours listen.

The other day I overheard a woman telling her friend, 'It is I who made my husband a millionaire.'
'And what was he before you married him?' asked the friend.
The woman replied, 'A multi-millionaire'.

A best man's speech should be like a mini-skirt: short enough to be interesting, but long enough to cover the bare essentials.

For twenty years, my wife and I were very happy. And then someone introduced us.

One day a man put an advert in the local newspaper:

'Wife wanted'. The next day he received a hundred letters. They all said the same thing: 'You can have mine.'

What's the difference between a tourniquet and a wedding ring? Nothing. They both stop a man's circulation.

Wife says to husband: 'No husband has ever been shot while doing the dishes.'

My friends say I am hen-pecked. But I think I am lucky to have my wife. She does everything for me. I don't even have to have my own opinions any more.

I married Miss Right. I just didn't know her first name was Always.

When I married my wife I got three rings – an engagement ring, a wedding ring and suffering.

There are two occasions on which a man doesn't understand a woman – before marriage and after it.

I asked my husband where he would like to go for our anniversary. 'Somewhere I have never been,' he replied. 'How about the kitchen?' I suggested, helpfully.

Marriage is like order envy. You choose, you look at what others have chosen, and you wish you had chosen what they have.

My best friend stole my husband but I got my revenge. I let her keep him.

Money

Always borrow money from a pessimist. He won't expect to get it back.

I wish the buck stopped here; I sure could use a few...

It's not hard to meet expenses... they're everywhere.

Bills travel through the mail at double the speed of cheques.

Why is it that bills never get lost in the mail, but cheques always do?

I pretend to work and my boss pretends to pay me.

Money is the root of all wealth.

There are two rules for being financially successful. Number 1: don't tell people rule number 2.

A fool and his money make a great party.

Money is better than poverty, if only for financial reasons.

The more a machine costs, the further you have to send it for repairs.

A suddenly wealthy friend of mine was a tried and trusted employee of a major international bank. Once he used to be trusted, now he is being tried.

Mothers

What would famous mothers have said to their offspring:

Christopher Columbus' mother: 'I don't care what you discovered, Chris, you still could have written.'

Napoleon's Mum: 'I know you are hiding your report inside your jacket. Take your hand out of there and give it to me. Mummy and Daddy won't be cross.'

Michelangelo's Mum: 'Do you have any idea how hard it is to get paint off the walls?'

Batman's Mum: 'Of course it is a lovely car, darling, but how are we going to afford the insurance?'

Superman's Mum: 'Your father and I have bought you a mobile, so you don't need to spend so much time in phone booths.'

Goldilock's Mum: 'Just how am I going to pay this bill for a broken chair?'

I confused my birth control pills with my valium. I have 10 children but I don't care.

The hardest thing about being a mother is controlling the temper tantrums. It's difficult not to have them in front of the children.

As a mother I am so proud to be part of a worldwide scientific experiment by men to see how long women can go without sleep.

I am so proud. The advice my son/daughter ignored is now being given to my grandchildren. There is a sense of delayed satisfaction in that, at least.

Things a mother would never say to her children:

'Don't sit so far away from the television – you won't
see a thing.'

'Don't worry. Skipping school is fine – I did it all the
time.'

'Yes, of course we can keep that stray dog and let's
look for a playmate for it.'

'I have run out of tissues – just use your sleeve.'

'Let's leave all the lights on. The house looks so much
more welcoming.'

'Don't worry about keeping your room tidy. I will clean
it up every day.'

Things I discovered as a mother:

Lego passes through the digestive tract of a child but
it takes its time.

One child's voice is more powerful in a restaurant
than that of 50 adults.

Children, like Super Glue, really are forever.

An 8-year old is better at starting a fire with a flint
rock than his father.

Plastic toys don't like ovens.

Somebody told me it took about six weeks to get back to
normal after you have had a baby. That somebody doesn't
know that once you are a mother normal is history.

I love being a mother. It's just the children I don't like.

Two mothers were talking about their sons. The first
said, 'My son is like a saint. He works hard, he doesn't
smoke and he hasn't looked at a woman in two years.'

The other woman, not to be outdone, said, 'Well, my son is a saint. Not only has he not looked at a woman in over three years, but he hasn't touched a drop of alcohol in all that time either.' 'You must be so proud!' said the first mother through gritted teeth. 'I certainly am,' replied the second mother, 'and when he gets out of jail next month, I am going to throw him a huge party and get all the chicks in town round.'

Why is it that other mums tell their daughters to look for a husband? They should be looking for a bachelor, shouldn't they?

My daughter is a dreadful flirt. When I told her so, she said she had been out with hundreds of boys and didn't let one of them kiss her. 'Which one was that?' I asked.

Opposite sex
Rules for finding a successful mate:
1 It is important to find a man who works around the house, occasionally cooks and cleans, and who has a job.
2 It is important to find a man who makes you laugh.
3 It is important to find a man who is dependable and doesn't lie.
4 It is important to find a man who worships your body.
5 It is vital that these four men never meet.

Not all men are annoying, some are dead.

Men are from Mars, women are arranging a return ticket.

Men can live without air for a few minutes, without water for a few days, without food for a month, and without new thoughts for years.

A woman's mind, like her underwear, is cleaner than a man's because she changes it more frequently.

Men will pay £2 for a £1 item they need.
Women will pay £1 for a £2 item they don't need but is on sale.

A woman has the last word in any argument.
Anything a man says after that is the beginning of a new argument.

A woman worries about the future until she gets a husband. A man never worries about the future until he gets a wife.

A woman knows all about her children, their dental appointments, romances, best friends, favourite foods, secret fears, hopes and dreams.
A man is vaguely aware of some short people living in the house.

Women use cosmetics to stop men from reading between the lines.

Politics

As Ronald Reagan said, politics is not a bad profession. If you succeed there are many rewards. If you disgrace yourself you can always write a book.

Q: Why should you bury politicians 100 feet deep?
A: Because deep down they are nice people.

Politicians are interested in people. Not that this is always a virtue. Fleas are interested in dogs.

Politicians are like nappies. They should be changed often.

Politicians lie, the media lies. But in a democracy, the lies are different.

Bureaucracy is like a septic tank. The big guys float to the top.

Why did the chicken cross the road?
- Karl Marx: It was an historical inevitability.
- Ronald Reagan: What chicken?
- Bill Clinton: I did not cross the road with that chicken.
- Bill Clinton again: Define the word cross.
- Martin Luther King Jnr: I envision a world in which chickens will be free to cross roads without being questioned.

A politician said to a woman: 'You look beautiful today.' The woman replied, 'Thanks but I can't say the same about you.' The politician countered, 'Of course you could if you could lie as well as I do.'

Deft Definitions

Definitions are also very useful for inserting a little light relief into a speech. These are listed in subject order and are suitable for all types of speeches and presentations.

Adolescent
A teenager who acts like a baby when you don't treat him like an adult.

Adult
A person who has stopped growing at both ends and started growing in the middle.

Alarm clock
A device used to wake up people who don't have small children.

Amnesia
Condition that enables a woman who has gone through labour to have sex again.

Ant
A busy insect that still finds time to go to picnics.

Appetizers
Little things you eat until you've lost your appetite.

Bachelor
A man with no ties – except those that need washing.

A man who has faults he doesn't know about yet.

Book
An object used to pass time while waiting for the TV repairman.

Boss
Someone who is early when you are late and late when you are early.

Buffet
A French word which means: 'Get up and get it yourself.'

Careful driver
One who has just spotted the police speed trap.

Charisma
That mysterious something that fat, bald billionaires have.

Child
Someone who can wash his hands without getting the soap wet.

Cigarette
A fire at one end, a fool at the other and a bit of tobacco in between.

College
A place where some pursue learning and others learn pursuing.

Conscience
The inner voice that warns us somebody is looking.

Consciousness
The annoying time between naps.

Cough
Something that you yourself can't help, but which everyone else does just to annoy you.

Courage
The art of being the only one who knows you're scared to death.

Credit card
What you use to buy today what you can't afford tomorrow while you're still paying for it yesterday.

Criminal
A bloke no different from the rest of us... except that he got caught.

Culture
A thin veneer easily soluble in alcohol.

Diet
A plan for putting off tomorrow what you put on today.

Discretion
Putting two and two together and keeping your mouth shut.

Dumb waiter
One who asks if the kids would care to order dessert.

Duty
Something one looks forward to without pleasure, does with reluctance, and boasts about afterwards.

Ecstasy
Discovering a second layer of chocolates under the first.

Eternity
The first 60 seconds of a blind date.

Etiquette
Knowing which finger to put in your mouth when you whistle for the waiter.

Expert
Someone who is called in at the last moment to share the blame.

Family
A group of people, no two of whom like their eggs cooked the same way.

Fancy restaurant
One that serves cold soup on purpose.

Feedback
The inevitable result when a baby doesn't appreciate the strained carrots.

Free speech
Using someone else's telephone.

Frustration
Trying to find your glasses without your glasses.

Gentleman
A man who holds the door open while his wife carries in the groceries.

Golf
A long walk punctuated by disappointments.

Gossip
The only thing that travels faster than e-mail.

The home
A place where a man can say what he likes – because no-one takes any notice of him anyway.

Husband
A man who wishes he had as much fun when he goes on business trips as his wife thinks he's having.

Influence
Something you think you have until you try to use it.

Key chain
A device that allows you to lose all your keys at the same time.

Leadership
The art of getting someone else to do something you want done because he wants to do it.

Manual
There are always three or more on a given item. One is on the shelf; someone has the others. The information you need is in the others.

Middle age
When knees buckle and belts don't.

Mobile phones
The only subject on which men boast about who's got the smallest.

Multitasking
Screwing up several things at once.

Office
A place where you can relax after your strenuous home-life.

Possibly
No in three syllables.

Recession
A period when we have to go without things our grandparents never heard of.

Riding
The art of keeping the horse between you and the ground.

Road map
Something that tells a motorist everything he wants to know – except how to fold it up agan.

School
A place where kids catch colds from each other so they can stay at home.

Semicolon
Half of a large intestine.

Semiconductors
Part-time band leaders.

Shin
A device for finding furniture in the dark.

Split second
The time between the lights changing and the driver behind you honking his horn.

Steering committee
Four people trying to park a car.

Tact
The ability to describe others as they see themselves.

Tomorrow
One of the greatest labour-saving devices of today.

Willpower
The ability to eat just one salted peanut.

chapter 2

Quotes

Quotations are another useful source of interesting content for speechmakers. They are effective since they can add impact and credibility to the point you are making, gain the audience's attention and sometimes make them laugh. Here are some key guidelines to help ensure that you use the right quote, at the right time, to the right audience:

Key guidelines:

- Don't use too many quotes: You will lessen their impact and your speech will become mechanical

- Limit them to one or two sentences: Audiences start switching off when they are read long quotes. Quotes are often most memorable when in a short, well-structured single sentence, e.g. 'I hear and I forget, I see and I remember, I do and I understand.'

- If you're not sure who said it, say so, but don't guess: Otherwise you risk undermining your entire speech. For example: 'Another form of reference material is statistics, but we must be careful with their use as we all recall the famous quote: 'There are three kinds of lies: lies, damned lies and statistics.'

- Make sure they are relevant: Just because you like a quote or think it is funny doesn't mean to say it will add to the effectiveness of your speech, it may just leave the audience wondering why on earth you have used it.

Finding quotations

Libraries and bookshops will, of course, stock treasuries of quotations. Consider using quotes from well-known humorous writers such as James Thurber, Charles Dickens, Mark Twain or Oscar Wilde.

Songwriters are another good source of quotable lines. You can track down the words of songwriters from books or librettos or some CD sleeves. Good songwriters to quote include W.S. Gilbert, Sammy Cahn and Noel Coward. Alternatively, refer to a good dictionary of popular music.

American quotations can be found among the sayings of every president, while politics, business, morality and determination to win against the odds are popular subjects.

Unless you are a great actor or orator, avoid any verse over four lines long. Five-line limericks, however, add humour, but be sure they are in good taste. Seek them out in a good poetry anthology.

Adapting quotations

The more you can relate your quotations to your audience and your subject matter, the more interested they will be. If the only quotation you can find is not very relevant or complimentary, adapt it. For example, at the wedding of a soldier you could start: 'According to the British Grenadiers, 'Some talk of Alexander, and some of Hercules, and others of Lysander and such great names as these.' But I would rather talk about Captain (groom's name).'

Below is a short selection of quotations for all occasions:

Age

Wrinkles should merely indicate where smiles have been.
Mark Twain, 19th century American author and humorist

Count your age with friends but not with years. *Anonymous*

You know you've reached middle age when your weight-lifting consists merely of standing up. *Bob Hope, 20th century American actor and comedian*

Thirty-five is a very attractive age. London society is full of women of the very highest birth who have, of their own free choice, remained thirty-five for years.
Oscar Wilde, 19th century Irish playwright and humorist

When I was young, I was told: 'You'll see, when you're fifty.' I am fifty and I haven't seen a thing. *Erik Satie, 19th century French composer*

Every man desires to live long but no man would be old.
Jonathan Swift, 18th century Anglo-Irish author

Growing old is like being increasingly penalized for a crime you haven't committed. *Anthony Powell, 20th century English author*

If I'd known I was gonna live this long, I'd have taken better care of myself. *Eubie Blake, 20th century American jazz musician*

An old man gives good advice in order to console himself for no longer being in a condition to set a bad example. *François La Rochefoucauld, 17th century French writer*

There's many a good tune played on an old fiddle. *Proverb*

Anger
When you enter into a house, leave the anger ever at the door. *Proverb*

Every minute you spend being angry with your partner is a waste of sixty seconds in which you could be enjoying yourselves. *Anonymous*

He that is angry is seldom at ease. *Proverb*

The greatest remedy for anger is delay. *Seneca, Roman statesman, 1st century philosopher and dramatist*

Animals
Odd things animals. All dogs look up at you. All cats look down at you. Only a pig looks at you as an equal. *Sir Winston Churchill, 20th century British Conservative Prime Minister and writer*

The giraffe must get up at six in the morning if it wants to have its breakfast in its stomach by nine. *Samuel Butler, 19th century English novelist*

The more one gets to know of men, the more one values dogs. *Alphonse Toussenel, 19th century French writer*

A door is what a dog is perpetually on the wrong side of. *Ogden Nash, 20th century American humorist*

The lion and the calf shall lie down together but the calf won't get much sleep. *Woody Allen, 20th century American comedian, actor, writer and director*

Appearance

If you actually like your passport photo you aren't well enough to travel. *Anonymous*

All that glitters is not gold. *Versions of this proverb appear in writing by Chaucer, William Shakespeare and Gray*

It is only shallow people who do not judge by appearances. *Oscar Wilde, 19th century Irish playwright and humorist*

He had but one eye, and the popular prejudice runs in favour of two. *Charles Dickens, 19th century English author*

I always say beauty is only sin deep. *Saki, 19th century Scottish-born writer*

Imprisoned in every fat man a thin one is wildly signalling to be let out. *Cyril Connolly, 20th century English writer*

The body of a young woman is God's greatest achievement... Of course, He could have built it to last longer but you can't have everything. *Neil Simon, 20th century American playwright*

Confidence is that quiet, assured feeling you have just before you fall flat on your face. *Anonymous*

Babies
A baby is an alimentary canal with a loud voice at one end and no responsibility at the other. *Ronald Reagan, 20th century American President*

A baby is God's opinion that the world should go on. *Carl Sandburg, 20th century American poet*

There are two things in this life for which we are never fully prepared: twins. *John Billings, 19th century American humorist*

People who say they sleep like a baby don't usually have one. *Leo J. Burke, 20th century American Catholic priest and teacher*

Architecture
No good building without a good foundation. *Proverb*

Architecture in general is frozen music. *Friedrich von Schelling (18th century)*

We shape our buildings, and afterwards our buildings shape us. *Winston Churchill, 1943*

Bachelors
Advice for those about to marry. Don't. *Punch magazine, 1845*

A bachelor gets tangled up with a lot of women in order to avoid getting tied up by one. *Helen Rowland, 20th century American writer*

A bachelor is a man who comes to work each morning from a different direction. *Sholom Aleichem. 19th century Russian-born Yiddish writer*

Business

Put all your eggs in one basket – and watch that basket. *Mark Twain, 19th century American author and humorist*

Buy in the cheapest market and sell in the dearest. *Proverb*

Drive your business, do not let it drive you. *Proverb*

It's a recession when your neighbour loses his job; it's a depression when you lose yours. *Harry S. Truman, 20th century American Democrat President*

Accept that some days you're the pigeon, and some days you're the statue. *Scott Adams, 20th century American cartoonist*

Nothing is as irritating as the chap who chats pleasantly to you while he's overcharging you. *Kin Hubbard, 19th century American writer*

I want a one-armed economist so that the guy could never make a statement and then say 'on the other hand...' *Harry S. Truman, 20th century American Democrat president*

In the business world an executive knows something about everything, a technician knows everything about something and the switchboard operator knows everything. *Harold Coffin, 20th century American journalist*

They usually have two tellers in my local bank, except when it's very busy, when they have one. *Rita Rudner, 20th century American comedienne*

Children

Anybody who hates children and dogs can't be all bad. *W.C. Fields, 20th century American actor and comedian*

There is only one beautiful child in the world and every mother has it. *Stephen Leacock, 20th century Canadian author and humorist*

He that has no children knows not what is love. *Proverb*

Children are poor men's riches. *Proverb*

You know your children are growing up when they stop asking where they come from and refuse to tell you where they are going. *P.J. O'Rourke, 20th century American political satirist and writer*

A mother's children are portraits of herself. *Anonymous*

I fear the seventh granddaughter and fourteenth grandchild becomes a very uninteresting thing – for it seems to me to go on like the rabbits in Windsor Park. *Queen Victoria (1819 – 1901)*

I have found the best way to give advice to your children is to find out what they want and then advise them to do it. *Harry S Truman, 20th century American Democrat president*

Cleaning your house while your kids are still growing is like shovelling the walk before it stops snowing. *Phyllis Diller, 20th century American comedienne*

Daughters
A son is a son till he gets him a wife, but a daughter's a daughter all the days of her life. *Proverb*

To a father growing old nothing is dearer than a daughter. *Euripides, Greek Playwright, 5th century BC*

He who has daughters is always a shepherd. *Proverb*

Deeds
Actions speak louder than words. *Proverb*

Our deeds determine us, as much as we determine our deeds. *George Eliot, 19th century British author*

Differences
All feet tread not in one shoe. *Proverb*

No dish pleases all palates alike. *Proverb*

We have become not a melting pot but a beautiful mosaic. Different people, different beliefs, different yearnings, different hopes, different dreams. *Jimmy Carter, 20th century American Democrat President*

Exercise
Start slow and taper off. *Walt Stack, 20th century American senior-citizen marathon runner*

Whenever I feel like exercise, I lie down until the feeling passes. *Robert M. Hutchins, 20th century American educator*

The only reason I would take up jogging is so that I could hear heavy breathing again. *Erma Bombeck, 20th century American writer and humorist*

I am pushing sixty. That is enough exercise for me. *Mark Twain, 19th century American author and humorist*

Experience
It is a silly fish that is caught twice with the same bait. *Proverb*

He is old enough to know worse. *Oscar Wilde, 19th century Irish playwright and humorist*

Experience is the best teacher. *Proverb*

Families
Happiness is having a large, loving, caring, close-knit family in another city. *George Burns, 20th century American comedian*

A family is a unit composed not only of children but of men, women, an occasional animal, and the common cold. *Ogden Nash, 20th century American humorist*

You don't choose your family. They are God's gift to you, as you are to them. *Desmond Tutu, 20th century South African cleric and political activist*

Friends
The only way to have a friend is to be one. *Ralph Waldo Emerson, 19th century American author, poet and philosopher*

Real friendship is shown in times of trouble; prosperity is full of friends. *Euripedes, Greek playwright, 5th century BC*

The proper office of a friend is to side with you when you are in the wrong. Nearly everybody will side with you when you are in the right. *Mark Twain, 19th century American writer and humorist*

The best mirror is an old friend. *Proverb*

Funerals
Dying is as natural as living. *Proverb*

Let no one weep for me or celebrate my funeral with mourning; for I live still, as I pass to and fro through the mouths of men. *Quintus Ennius, Roman poet, 2nd century BC*

The grave is but a covered bridge leading from light to light, through a brief darkness! *Henry Wadsworth Longfellow, 19th century American poet*

Generation gap
It is the one war in which everyone changes sides. *Cyril Connolly, 20th century English writer*

Grown-ups never understand anything for themselves, and it is tiresome for children to be always and forever explaining things to them. *Antoine de Saint-Exupéry, 20th century French aviator and writer*

When I was a boy of 14, my father was so ignorant I could hardly stand to have him around. But when I got to be 21, I was astonished at how much the old man had learned in seven years. *Attributed to Mark Twain, 19th century American writer and humorist*

Happiness
All happiness is in the mind. *Proverb*

The joy of the heart makes the face fair. *Proverb*

He is not rich that possesses much, but he that is content with what he has. *Proverb*

Content lodges oftener in cottages than palaces. *Proverb*

Health and wealth
I wish you health; I wish you wealth; I wish you gold in store; I wish you heaven when you die; what could I wish you more? *Anonymous*

Never go to a doctor whose office plants have died. *Erma Bombeck, 20th century American humorist*

I don't believe in vitamin pills. I swear by men, darling – and as many as possible. *Joan Collins, 20th century English actress and author*

Home

There is no place like home after the other places close. *Anonymous*

Home is the place where, when you have to go there, they have to take you in. *Robert Frost, 20th century American poet*

Home is where the television is. *Anonymous*

Honesty

The best measurement of a man's honesty isn't his income tax return. It's the zero adjustment on his bathroom scales. *Arthur C. Clarke, 20th century English writer*

Honesty is the best policy, but it is not the cheapest. *Mark Twain, 19th century American writer and humorist*

An honest man's word is as good as his bond. *Proverb*

Honour

It is a worthier thing to deserve honour than to possess it. *Proverb*

He that desires honour is not worthy of honour. *Proverb*

Hope

In the land of hope there is never any winter. *Proverb*

When one door shuts another opens. *Proverb*

Hope springs eternal in the human breast. *Proverb*

Hospitality
The guest of the hospitable learns hospitality. *Proverb.*

Welcome is the best dish. *Proverb*

Husbands
Trust your husband, adore your husband, and get as much as you can in your own name. *Joan Rivers, 20th century American comedienne*

A husband's last words are always, 'OK, buy it! *N.P.Willis, 19th century American writer*

The husband who wants a happy marriage should learn to keep his mouth shut and his checkbook open. *Groucho Marx, 20th century American comedian*

Kindness
You have it easily in your power to increase the sum total of this world's happiness. How? By giving a few words of sincere appreciation to someone who is lonely or discouraged. Perhaps you will forget tomorrow the kind words you say today, but the recipient may cherish them over a lifetime. *Dale Carnegie, 20th century American public speaker*

One of the most difficult things to give away is kindness – it is usually returned. *Anonymous*

One can always be kind to people about whom one cares nothing. *Oscar Wilde, 19th century Irish playwright and humorist*

The little unremembered acts of kindness and love are the best parts of a person's life. *William Wordsworth, 19th century English poet*

Laziness
Anybody who isn't pulling his weight is probably pushing his luck. *Anonymous*

The devil finds work for idle hands to do. *Anonymous*

Life
Life is what happens to you when you're making other plans. *Robert Balzer*

If you can't convince them, confuse them. *Harry S. Truman, 33rd President of the USA*

Let the refining and improving of your own life keep you so busy that you have little time to criticize others. *H. Jackson Brown, American author of 'Life's Little Instruction Manual'*

Life ... is like a cup of tea; the more heartily we drink, the sooner we reach the dregs. *J.M. Barrie, 19th century Scottish playwright*

Life is something to do when you can't get to sleep. *Fran Lebowitz, 20th century American humorist and essayist*

Life is like playing a violin solo in public and learning the instrument as one goes on. *Edward Bulwer-Lytton, 19th century English politician and novelist*

The only thing I regret about my life is the length of it. If I had to live my life again I'd make all the same mistakes – only sooner. *Tallulah Bankhead, 20th century American actress*

Losing
The only time losing is more fun than winning is when you're fighting temptation. *Tom Wilson, 20th century American actor, writer and comedian*

He that loses anything and gets wisdom by it is a gainer by the loss. *Proverb*

Losing one glove is sorrow enough
But nothing compared with the pain
Of losing one glove
Discarding the other
Then finding the first one again.
Piet Hein, 20th century Danish poet and inventor

You cannot lose what you never had. *Proverb*

Love
Give her two red roses, each with a note. The first note says: 'For the woman I love', and the second: 'For my best friend.' *Anonymous*

True love never grows old. *Proverb*

The best and the most beautiful things in the world cannot be seen or even touched. They must be felt with the heart. *Helen Keller, 20th century American deaf and blind author, activist and lecturer*

Women are meant to be loved, not understood.
Oscar Wilde, 19th century Irish playwright and humorist

And all for love, and nothing for reward. *Edmund Spenser, 16th century English poet*

Marriage
A good marriage is like a casserole, only those responsible for it really know what goes in it. *Anonymous*

Marriage resembles a pair of shears, so joined that they cannot be separated; often moving in opposite directions, yet always punishing any one who comes between them. *Sydney Smith, 19th century English preacher*

All marriages are happy. It's living together afterwards that is difficult. *Anonymous*

Every mother generally hopes that her daughter will snag a better husband than she managed to do...but she's certain that her boy will never get as great a wife as his father did. *Anonymous*

Marriage is like a violin. After the music is over, you still have the strings. *Anonymous*

Marriage is a great institution, but I'm not ready for an institution. *Mae West, 20th century American actress*

Better to have loved a short man than never to have loved a tall. *Anonymous*

An archaeologist is the best husband a woman can have; the older she gets the more interested he is in her. *Agatha Christie, 20th century English author*

Marriage is like a bank account. You put it in, you take it out, you lose interest. *Irwin Corey, 20th century American humorist*

A toast to sweethearts. May all sweethearts become married couples and may all married couples remain sweethearts. *Anonymous*

Marriage halves our griefs, doubles our joys and quadruples our expenses. *Proverb*

Marriage is a matter of give and take, but so far I haven't been able to find anybody who'll take what I have to give. *Cass Daley, 20th century American comedienne*

Marriage is like a cage; one sees the birds outside desperate to get in; and those inside desperate to get out. *Michel de Montaigne, 16th century French writer*

I've been married so many times my certificate now reads: 'To whom it may concern.' *Mickey Rooney, 20th century American actor*

A man without a wife is but half a man. *Proverb*

If it were not for the presents, an elopement would be preferable. *George Ade, 20th century American humorist and dramatist*

It is a truth universally acknowledged that a single man in possession of a good fortune must be in want of a wife. *Jane Austen, 18th century English author*

Before I got married I had six theories about bringing up children; and now I have six children and no theories. *John Wilmot, 2nd Earl of Rochester (1647-80)*

Marriage is popular because it combines the maximum of temptation with the maximum of opportunity. *George Bernard Shaw, 20th century Irish playwright*

A good marriage would be between a blind wife and a deaf husband. *Attributed to Michel de Montaigne, 16th century French writer*

To keep your marriage brimming
With love in the loving cup,
Whenever you're wrong, admit it,
Whenever you're right, shut up.
Ogden Nash, 20th century American poet and humorist

It's a woman's business to get married as soon as possible, and a man's to keep unmarried as long as he can. *George Bernard Shaw, 20th century Irish playwright 16th century*

Marriage is a wonderful invention, but then again, so is the bicycle repair kit. *Billy Connolly, 20th century Scottish comedian*

Never go to bed mad. Stay up and fight. *Phyllis Diller, 20th century American comedienne*

Men

My mother said it was simple to keep a man – you must be a maid in the living room, a cook in the kitchen and a whore in the bedroom. I said I'd hire the other two and take care of the bedroom bit. *Jerry Hall, 20th century American model*

I married beneath me. All women do.
Nancy Astor, 20th century American-born British politician

Boys will be boys, and so will a lot of middle-aged men.
Kin Hubbard, 19th century American writer

It's not the men in my life, but the life in my men.
Mae West, 20th century American actress

The more I see of men, the more I like dogs. *Mme Roland, 18th century French revolutionary*

Women's faults are many
But men have only two –
Everything they say
And everything they do.
Anonymous

Men and women

When women go wrong, men go right after them.
Mae West, 20th century American actress

Whatever women do, they must do twice as well as men to be thought half as good. Luckily, this is not difficult.
Charlotte Whitton, 20th century Canadian feminist

A little incompatibility is the spice of life, particularly if he has income and she is pattable. *Ogden Nash, 20th century American poet and humorist*

You think that you are Ann's suitor; that you are the pursuer and she the pursued... Fool: it is you who are the pursued, the marked down quarry, the destined prey. *George Bernard Shaw, 20th century Irish playwright*

A woman's mind is cleaner than a man's; she changes it more often. *Oliver Herford, 20th century British-born American writer and poet*

Music
I assure you that the typewriting machine, when played with expression, is not more annoying than the piano when played by a sister or near relation. *Oscar Wilde, 19th century Irish playwright and humorist*

If you're in jazz and more than ten people like you, you're labelled commercial. *Herbie Mann, 20th century American jazz flautist*

Opera is when a guy gets stabbed in the back and, instead of bleeding, he sings. *Ed Gardner, 20th century American comedian*

I only know two tunes. One of them is 'Yankee Doodle' and the other isn't. *Ulysses S. Grant, 19th century American Union General and President*

There are two golden rules for an orchestra: start

together and finish together. The public doesn't give a damn what goes on in between. *Thomas Beecham, 20th century English conductor*

I can't listen to too much Wagner, ya know? I start to get the urge to conquer Poland. *Woody Allen, 20th century American comedian, actor, writer and director*

Neighbours
No one is rich enough to do without his neighbours. *Proverb*

To have a good neighbour is to find something precious. *Proverb*

A near neighbour is better than a far-dwelling kinsman. *Proverb*

Parents
The heart of a mother is a deep abyss at the bottom of which you will always find forgiveness. *Honoré de Balzac, 19th century French author*

No one in the world can take the place of your mother. Right or wrong, from her viewpoint you are always right. She may scold you for little things, but never for the big ones. *Harry S. Truman, 20th century American Democrat President*

A Jewish man with parents alive is a fifteen-year-old boy, and will remain a fifteen-year-old boy until they die! *Philip Roth, 20th century American author*

There's only one pretty child in the world, but every mother has it. *Proverb*

Parents are the bones on which children cut their teeth. *Peter Ustinov, 20th century British-born writer, actor, dramatist and raconteur*

Public speaking
It usually takes me more than three weeks to prepare a good impromptu speech. *Mark Twain, 19th century American author and humorist*

Half the world is composed of people who have something to say and can't, and the other half who have nothing to say and keep on saying it. *Robert Frost, 19th century American poet*

Blessed is the man who having nothing to say, abstains from giving us wordy evidence of the fact. *George Eliot, 19th century English writer*

The human brain is a marvellous thing. It whirrs away continuously from the moment you are born and carries on even while you are asleep... but the moment you open your mouth to make a speech... *Anonymous*

I do not object to people looking at their watches when I am speaking. But I strongly object when they start shaking them to make sure they are still going. *Norman Birkett (Lord Birkett), 20th century English barrister and judge*

Speeches are like babies – easy to conceive but hard to deliver. *Aristotle, 4th century BC Greek philosopher*

Retirement
It is true that hard work never killed anybody, but I figured, why take the chance? *Ronald Reagan, 20th century American actor and Republican President*

Retirement is wonderful. It's doing nothing without worrying about getting caught at it. *Gene Perret, 20th century American writer and humorist*

I will not retire while I've still got my legs and my make-up box. *Bette Davis, 20th century American actress*

The best time to start thinking about your retirement is before the boss does. *Anonymous*

Work is the curse of the drinking classes. *Oscar Wilde, 19th century Irish playwright and humorist*

Anyone can do any amount of work provided it isn't the work he is supposed to be doing at that moment. *Robert Benchley, 20th century American writer and humorist*

Second marriage
I'm not so old, and not so plain, and I'm quite prepared to marry again. *W.S. Gilbert, 20th century English playwright and humorist*

The triumph of hope over experience. *Dr Samuel Johnson, 18th century English writer*

Self-deprecating

I will try to follow the advice that a university president once gave a prospective commencement speaker. 'Think of yourself as the body at an Irish wake,' he said. 'They need you in order to have the party, but no-one expects you to say very much.' *Anthony Lake, 20th century US National Security advisor*

I have often wished I had time to cultivate modesty... But I am too busy thinking about myself. *Dame Edith Sitwell, 20th century English poet, critic and biographer*

The English instinctively admire any man who has no talent and is modest about it. *James Agate, 20th century English drama critic*

Success

If at first you don't succeed, try, try, a couple of times more. Then quit: there's no sense in making a fool of yourself. *W.C. Fields, 20th century American actor and comedian*

To succeed –
Early to bed, early to rise,
Never get tight, and – advertise.
Anonymous

Failure teaches success. *Proverb*

Success is not measured by what one brings, but rather by what one leaves. *Anonymous*

Whom the gods wish to destroy they first call promising.
Cyril Connolly, 20th century English writer

It takes twenty years to make an overnight success.
Eddie Cantor, 20th century American entertainer

Temptation
It's hard to fight temptation. There is always the nagging
thought that it might not happen again. *Anonymous*

I can resist everything except temptation. *Oscar Wilde,*
19th century Irish playwright and humorist

If you can't be good, be careful. *Proverb*

All the things I really like to do are either illegal,
immoral or fattening. *Alexander Woollcott, 20th century*
American author and critic

The only way to get rid of temptation is to yield to it.
Oscar Wilde, 19th century Irish playwright and humorist

Thanks
Do not forget little kindnesses and do not remember
small faults. *Proverb*

At times our own light goes out and is rekindled by a
spark from another person. Each of us has cause to
think with deep gratitude of those who have lighted the
flame within us. *Albert Schweitzer, 20th century German*
humanitarian, organist and doctor

Time

Time is a great healer. *Proverb*

The golden age was never the present age. *Proverb*

Time is God's way of keeping everything from happening at once. *Anonymous*

Wealth

A rich man is nothing but a poor man with money. *W.C.Fields, 20th century American actor and comedian*

He does not possess wealth; it possesses him. *Benjamin Franklin, 18th century American politician and scientist*

The meek shall inherit the earth, but not the mineral rights. *John Paul Getty, 20th century American business tycoon*

The rich man knows not who is his friend. *Proverb*

Money is better than poverty, if only for financial reasons. *Woody Allen, 20th century American actor, comedian, director and writer*

Money won't buy happiness, but it will pay the salaries of a large research staff to study the problem. *Bill Vaughan, 20th century American writer*

If you would know what the Lord God thinks of money, you have only to look at those to whom He gave it. *Maurice Baring, 20th century English writer*

'My boy,' he says, 'always try to rub up against money, for if you rub up against money long enough, some of it may rub off on you.' *Damon Runyon, 20th century American writer*

Annual income twenty pounds, annual expenditure nineteen nineteen and six, result happiness. Annual income twenty pounds, annual expenditure twenty pounds nought and six, result misery. *Charles Dickens, 19th century English writer*

A bank is a place that will lend you money if you can prove that you don't need it. *Bob Hope, 20th century American comedian*

Wisdom
Trouble brings experience and experience brings wisdom. *Proverb*

Wisdom is a treasure for all time. *Proverb*

Wives
I have learned that there are only two things necessary to keep one's wife happy. First, let her think she's having her way. And second, let her have it. *Lyndon B. Johnson, 20th century American Democrat President*

A good wife and health is a man's best wealth. *Proverb*

Apologise to a man if you're wrong, but to your wife even if you're right. *Anonymous*

Women

A woman's place is in the wrong. *Attributed to James Thurber, 20th century American writer and cartoonist*

The only premarital thing girls don't do these days is the cooking. *Omar Sharif, 20th century Egyptian actor*

Brigands demand your money or your life; women require both. *Samuel Butler, 19th century English writer*

Happiness? A good cigar, a good meal, and a good woman – or a bad woman.It depends upon how much happiness you can handle. *Attributed to George Burns, 20th century American comedian*

Women represent the triumph of matter over mind, just as men represent the triumph of mind over morals. *Oscar Wilde, 19th century Irish playwright and humorist*

chapter 3

Stories & Anecdotes

As the saying goes, reality is often stranger, and funnier, than fiction. Whereas joke-telling relies to a certain extent on a degree of natural aptitude, most people are able to recount stories, either of events that have happened to them or to others. When combined with dynamic delivery, in terms of use of voice, facial expressions and body language, stories and anecdotes can be a lot funnier than jokes. An added advantage is that we find it a lot easier to recall and tell stories than we do to memorize and tell jokes, where we often trip over the punch line.

Although you can collect stories and anecdotes from reference books such as this, often the most effective ones are from your own experience. Ask yourself: 'What is the subject of this speech or presentation?' and then: 'What are some of my more memorable experiences with the subject of the speech?' These two simple questions will often unearth excellent and relevant stories.

It might help to explain what an anecdote actually is. One definition reveals it as 'a short account of some interesting or humorous incident.' An anecdote is not a long joke. It is a brief tale that should be based on real incident, real life, actual persons, real places.

Your anecdote should not only be short, interesting or humorous, it should actually have a point. It is sometimes described as a 'bottom up' narrative. What this means is that the point, truth, fact or sentiment – whatever you are trying to communicate or illustrate – comes in the final paragraph. If you remember this, you will avoid rambling, always a danger of anecdotes. Remember, too, that anecdotes are essentially oral in nature. Don't write a lengthy essay and read it out. That would be a lecture, and will make the account sound less sincere. Speak from the heart, not the book or page. It is fine to use quotes but do so sparingly and don't make your anecdote a loosely linked collection of quotes and proverbs you looked up the night before!

When thinking about your anecdote, keep the following words in mind: appropriate, believable, personal, relevant, interesting and short. As with all aspects of speech making, think about who will be listening and adjust your language and content accordingly. Think about the occasion, then think back to your own experiences and the people, places, incidents, sentiments involved, and then consider how all these can come together to illustrate a point and mark the occasion.

Think past, people, places, point, punch line (PPPPP). You are more likely to remember the details if they come from your own past. There is nothing worse when telling a joke or recounting an anecdote than drying up half way through or forgetting the punch line. Once you have spoken your punch line, it is time to close.

If you are recounting dialogue, don't fall into the 'he said, she said and then he said and then I said' trap. Try limiting dialogue to two or three exchanges. Otherwise you are in danger of losing the audience's interest and making your account sound like something you tell friends in a pub rather than relate to an assembled audience.

A useful mantra when trying to think up anecdotes for inclusion in your speech is:

Past events

Personalities and People

Places

Point

Punch line

(and mind your Ps and Qs, too!)

Anecdotes check list:

- **A**ppropriate, amusing and audible (is it going to offend? Will it entertain? Can they hear you?)
- **N**ames (have you got them right and remembered them or written on a prompt card?)
- **E**vents (is your anecdote based on an interesting incident?)
- **C**oncrete (include concrete details rather than abstract ideas)
- **D**etails and descriptions (make them real, make them play a role or drop them)
- **O**ral (remember this is an oral tradition; make it a short story not a lengthy lecture)
- **T**ime (keep it short and punchy or you will lose attention and steal other people's time)
- **E**nding (this is the important part – the conclusion in both senses)

Over the next few pages you will find some questions that are intended to inspire you and help you come up with personal anecdotes for both social and business speeches.

Christenings and baptisms
Appropriate for a godparent

As a godparent you may be called upon to make a speech during the celebration that follows a christening or baptism. If a baby or young child is being christened, your anecdote will probably refer to your relationship with the parents and how you came to be chosen as a godparent. The point of your anecdote is likely to be how much your friendship with the parent(s) means to you and how you have agreed to extend that relationship into the future by playing an instructive and active role in the life of the child, as his or her spiritual mentor. The 'why' and 'how' of this can form the first part of your story, in this case your joint story or history (or his 'n' hers story...).

Prompter questions:
- How long have you known the parent(s)?
- How did you meet?
- Did a special incident bring you together?
- Why have you agreed to take on the role as spiritual mentor?
- Why do you think you were chosen?
- What does being a godparent mean to you?
- What role have your own godparents played in your life?
- In the event that your godchild is older, what role will you play in his or her life now?

Bar and Bat Mitzvah

If you are choosing a story for a bar or bat mitzvah speech remember that the occasion celebrates the family and the broader Jewish community, as well as the bar or bat mitzvah themselves. An appropriate anecdote might be one in which the boy or girl's role within the family is highlighted – for example, if the candidate has always been the family musician or scholar, you might recall an occasion in the past in which he or she played the leading role, and relate it to their maturing identity as they officially enter adulthood. The story should refer to their special qualities. If you are not a family member you might include a brief, affectionate account of how you came to be friends. This is an occasion of deep spiritual meaning, so steer clear of 'hilarious' stories: gentle humour will be more suitable.

Prompter questions

- If you are not a family member, how did you come to know the family, and the bar/bat mitzvah?
- What are the bar/bat mitzvah's distinctive qualities and how can you talk about them?
- Has the bar/bat mitzvah taken part in community events?
- If you know the bar/bat mitzvah's parents, are there stories you can use to compare the two generations?
- What do you wish for the bar/bat mitzvah's future?
- What can you remember (tactfully!) of the bar/bat mitzvah's early childhood?
- Are there aspects of your own bar/bat mitzvah that you can relate to today's occasion?

Confirmation

Appropriate for godparent, parent, sibling or close family friend

If you are to tell an anecdote at a confirmation party, remember that the occasion marks a confirmation of faith, an admittance to full membership of the Church. However, although your anecdote should acknowledge this important step in the life of the 'candidate', it can also include some gentle humour and amusing nostalgia. It is an opportunity for you to talk about the experiences and events in the years leading up to this day, to look back at the candidate's past achievements and experiences and forward to those to come. You can also refer to all those, including yourself, who have been involved in the candidate's progression to this key stage in their religious life.

Prompter questions:
- What does the day mean to the candidate (and those present)?
- How long have you known the candidate?
- What role have you played in his/her life?
- What role will you play in the future?
- What was he/she like when younger?
- What has he/she brought to your life, the life of his/her parents and siblings, and others?
- What scholarly, sporting, artistic achievements can you highlight?
- What challenges has he/she overcome to get to this point in his or her life?
- What amusing events, characteristics, foibles can you relate?

What did your own confirmation mean to you?

Coming of age – 18th or 21st birthday
Appropriate for godparent, parent, guardian

Milestone birthdays present parents, grandparents, guardians, godparents and close friends with an ideal and memorable opportunity to congratulate young adults on their achievements to date, to look back at their past fondly and to wish them well in the future. There is usually no shortage of anecdotal material, some of it mildly and possibly humorously critical, but try not to cause embarrassment or offence. Many young people have yet to develop their defence mechanisms and are easily embarrassed, particularly in front of their peers. Keep your anecdote a gentle mix of memories, nostalgia, humour, fact, congratulation and celebration. You could also use photographs, video or audio material as props.

Prompter questions:
- What did he/she look like as a baby?
- Was he/she charming or challenging?
- What were his/her first words?
- Was there anything he/she did when small that would make a particularly humorous story?
- What were the highlights (and lowlights) of his/her adolescence?
- What special moments have you shared?
- What achievements can you describe without embarrassing him/her too much?
- What character traits do you particularly admire in him/her?
- What does the future hold for them at this stage?
- What role would you like to play in their next planned step on his/her journey to adulthood?

Weddings (including hen and stag nights)
Appropriate for best man or woman, or close friend

If you will be speaking at pre-wedding parties and the wedding itself, make sure you use different stories (some of the guests will be present at both) that are appropriate for the occasion. Hen and stag nights, or bachelor parties as they are sometimes called, offer the perfect forum for amusing anecdotes to be told in a relaxed atmosphere, usually among a peer group rather than in the company of older relatives and friends. On both occasions, resist the temptation to make them highly embarrassing, revealing or painful. Keep your anecdote short, light-hearted, humorous and enjoyable, with no repercussions. As best man (or woman), you should remain aware of your responsibility to make things go smoothly and without incident and include your anecdote in this.

Prompter questions:
- How do you know the bride or groom?
- Is there a particular incident from your friendship or their early romantic history you could relate, without causing too much embarrassment?
- Does he/she have any characteristics or foibles that would make a good story?
- Were you present when the couple met?
- Are there any particularly humorous incidents from their relationship you can narrate?
- Why do you think they will make a perfect couple?
- What role do you hope to play in their future?
- What advice can you offer for their marriage to be a happy one?

Wedding anniversary
Best man or bridesmaid

Wedding anniversary speeches and anecdotes can be delivered by a number of different people, including close members or friends of the family, the best man or bridesmaid, or, naturally, the husband or wife. Nostalgic and humorous anecdotes can be very appropriate for such occasions, as the couple and their family and friends look back over the years, remembering the wedding day and all that has happened since. You might even use an old photograph or two (but not several) to illustrate a particular incident or to talk about the big day itself. Quotes are also both appropriate and useful.

Prompter questions:
- Have you known the couple longer than anyone else present?
- What is special about your relationship with them?
- Is there a particularly humorous, gently embarrassing, wonderfully romantic incident from the wedding (or since the event) you can talk about?
- Are there particular sensitivities you should be aware of? (For example if theirs is a second marriage, or there are step-children you should think about.)
- Can you make the content of your anecdote appropriate for the relevant 'milestone' anniversary, e.g. diamond, golden, silver?
- Can you make effective or humorous use of old photographs or props?
- Can you involve other people in your story, ask others to contribute a few words about the big day, or introduce a surprise guest?

Retirement or leaving party
Appropriate for boss or long-standing colleague

Anecdotes told at leaving or retirement parties should focus on the person rather than the business. They are not occasions upon which to discuss sales figures, unless a particularly relevant incident brings humour or special congratulations with it. It is important to bring emotion to the event. Try to stand close to the person leaving or retiring, and recount your anecdote with warmth and sincerity. Memorize your story to help with this – don't read from a script. Your anecdote should be used to praise, congratulate and thank the person involved, wishing them well in the next stage of their careers or lives. And keep it relatively short and succint. Remember, too, that the event is not about you. Attention should be focused entirely on the person leaving.

Prompter questions:
- How long have you worked with the person who is leaving?
- What special, interesting, humorous events/moments/incidents in your professional or personal lives have you shared?
- What are the qualities of the person you most admire?
- What positive role in your own professional career (or that of others) has he or she played?
- What will you miss most about them in the workplace?
- What will you miss least?
- What are they planning to do next and what skills can you highlight that will make this a success?

Funerals

Funeral speeches and anecdotes are among the hardest things we can be asked to do. It may make it easier, and less daunting, to see the task as a way of celebrating a life rather than mourning its ending. Anecdotes can offer a glimpse of a life that others have not seen. You may be the only person who shared a particular period of the deceased's life, or experienced the incident you recount. Imagine it as a photograph, a word-picture you are handing round, one that can be treasured by those present after the ceremony. Funeral anecdotes can be told with quiet laughter, affectionate nostalgia and bring to the proceedings a sense of affirmation of a life lived.

Prompter questions:

- Have you known the deceased longer than anyone else or have you shared a part of their life that others haven't?
- Can you offer a different glimpse into their life or shed a different light on their personality?
- How would the person like to be remembered?
- What did you or others really like about them?
- What made them a special person?
- What was the highlight of the time you shared together?
- Can you talk about a time when they were really happy?
- Can you introduce gentle humour into the ceremony with your story? Would that be appropriate? Would the person have enjoyed hearing what you have to say?
- How can you paint a lasting memory for those present to take away with them?

Sales meeting or sales conference
Appropriate for Sales Team Managers, Sales Directors, Presenters
Anecdotes told at business meetings or sales conferences are most effective if kept short and succinct, particularly if they are one of many presentations to be given. You can make your salient point or points (but limit them!) with humour, offering a little light relief while at the same time delivering an important message, whether motivational, congratulatory or constructively critical. You might want to use a few props, such as a flip chart or audiovisual material, but do so in an engaging, humorous, rather than academic or very serious, way. Ask one or more of the delegates to help or participate, maybe doing some role play based on members of the team, management or customer base. Engage interest through entertainment. Make your anecdote different and memorable. It may be the one the delegates go home thinking about.

Prompter questions:
- Where will your anecdote come in the running order of speeches and presentations?
- How alert/tired/bored/motivated will your audience be?
- What are your (maximum 3) key points?
- What are the dynamics of your team – who is the leader, the alpha salesperson, the peace-keeper etc?
- Who would be a good person to select to help you?
- Does your team generally respond to humour?
- Have there been any particularly successful or unsuccessful presentations to bear in mind?
- What past achievements can you highlight?
- Do you have to deliver a difficult message?

Opening a new building

If you are asked to speak at the inauguration of a new building, you can bring gentle humour or nostalgia to the formality of the occasion with your anecdote. It may be appropriate to think back to the building being replaced and talk of your existing, past relationship (if relevant) and future, potential one. Quotes about buildings and architecture can be helpful, too. Discuss and describe the structure itself, the people involved, how it came to be built and what role it will play in the village, town or city in which it has been erected. Focus your attention on the building and its importance in your life rather than vice versa. This should also help with any nerves about the task.

Prompter questions:

- What does it mean to you to have been asked to speak at the event?
- How were you involved in the building being replaced?
- How were you instrumental in the new one being built?
- What role did the old building play in your past (childhood, adolescence, career etc)?
- How did those present contribute?
- Did anything particularly challenging or humorous occur during the construction?
- Is there a particularly appropriate quote you can use?
- What does the building mean to the community?

Index

Notes

Use these last pages to make notes to help you with your speech, such as any good tips, quotes or jokes that you have heard recently.